This book belongs to

_____

For my husband.

When this life tries to pull me under,
you always keep my head above water.
Thank you for showing up for us.
You are my greatest adventure.

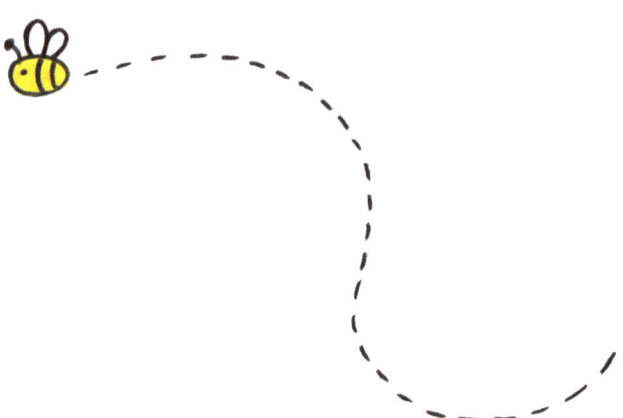

Library of Congress Control Number: 2025918218

Hi. My name is Audra.

I do not speak.

I'm autistic and unique.

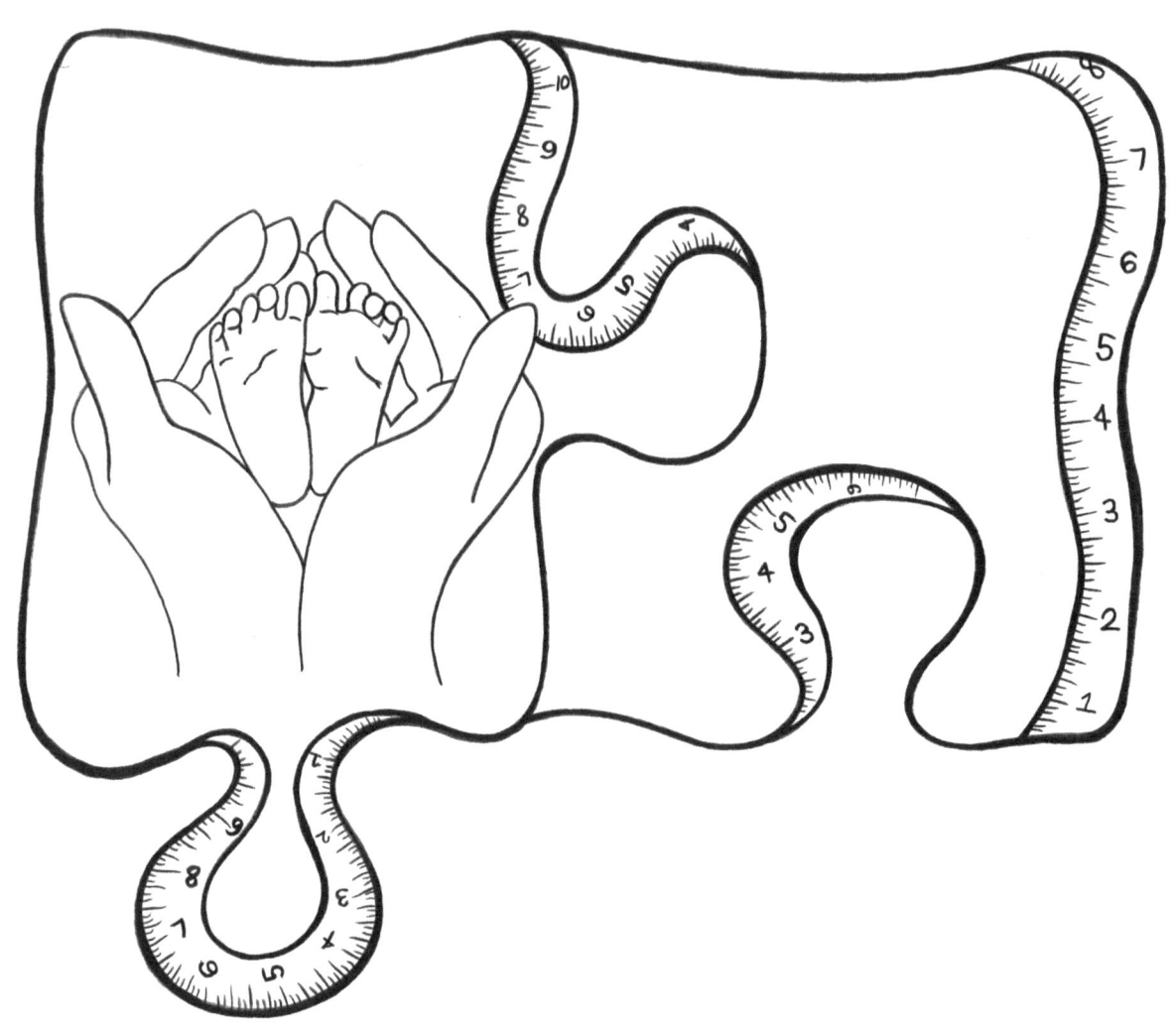

I started like you,

a tiny baby that quickly grew.

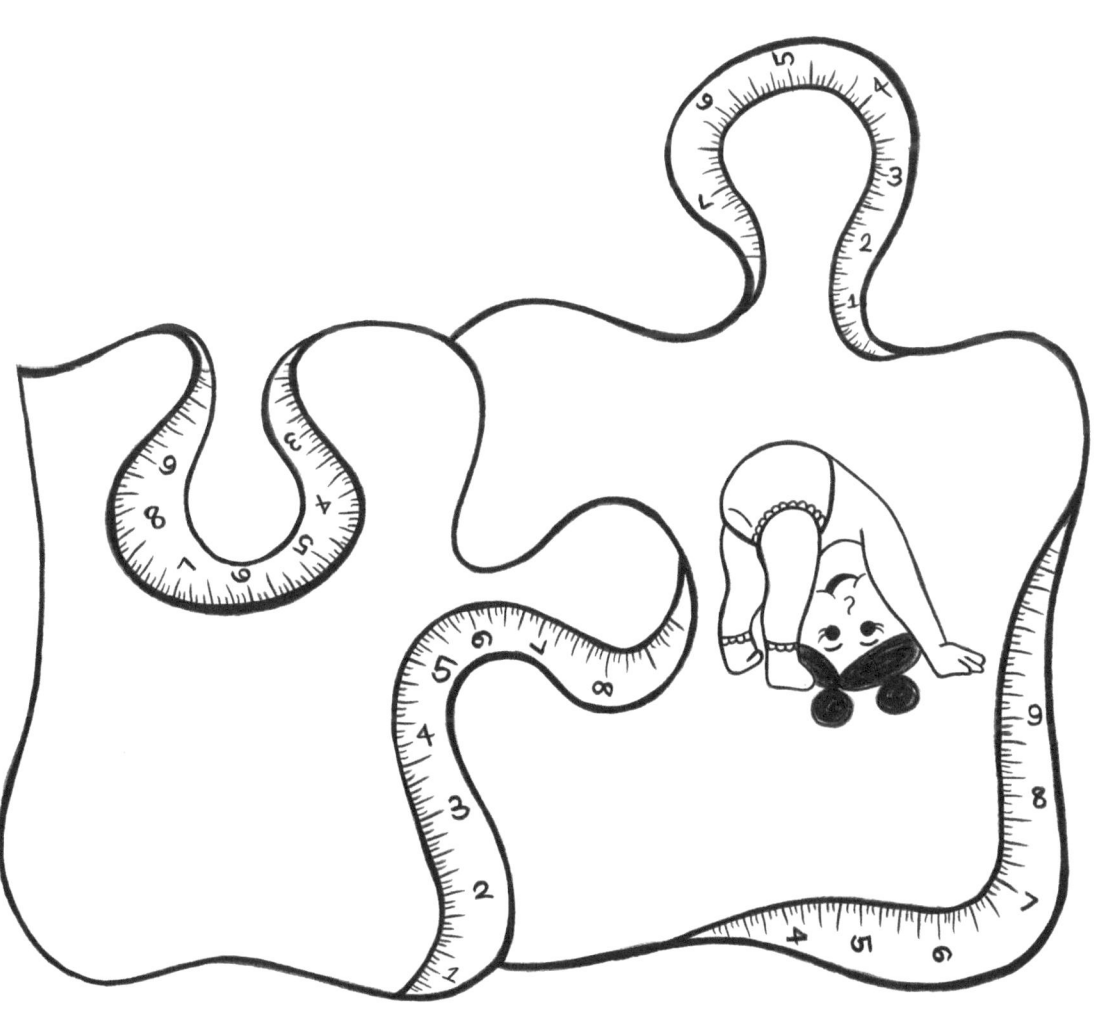

Though

I never

said my

first word,

I can still make sounds and be heard.

I laugh and sometimes cry,

but I cannot tell you why.

I communicate
in a different way,

by taking your hand
throughout the day.

I love the outdoors and long car rides.

But turn me loose and watch my strides.

I don't use a fork to eat,

but use my fingers for almost any treat.

I feel joy and pain,

but for you and me it's not the same.

When I am happy I flap my hands

and jump around and scream and dance.

When I fall down and bump my knee,

I don't shed a tear or two or three.

I show love with a simple touch.

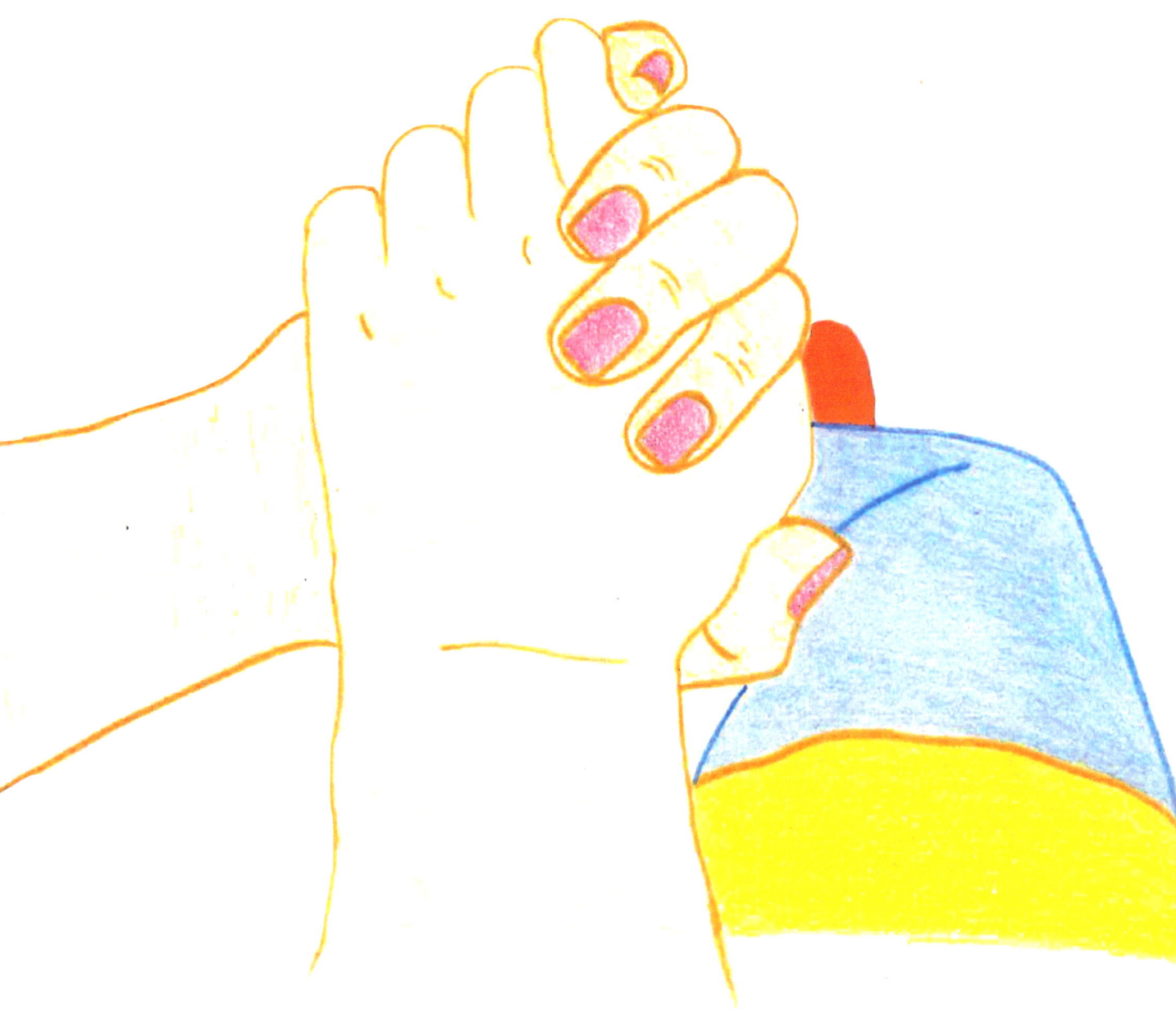

No need for words to prove how much.

There are many others just like me,

who want to be understood and be free...

...to be ourselves outside our space,

and belong anywhere and any place.

With a little love and patience too,

we can be friends, me and you.

And when you get the chance
to make the choice,

choose to be someone's voice.

It can change their entire day,

to the brightest bright

from a gloomy gray.

Remember kindness matters
and costs nothing.

So thank you for reading
and letting me be seen.

www.ingramcontent.com/pod-product-compliance
Lightning Source LLC
Chambersburg PA
CBHW041500120626
46547CB00003B/483

9 7 9 8 2 1 8 7 6 8 2 5 6